Plan for seizing and carrying to N. Y.

Coll. Wm. Goffe

The Regicide

by

Franklin B. Hough, M. D.

Albany.

1855.

PLAN
FOR SEIZING AND CARRYING TO NEW-YORK
COLL. WM. GOFFE
THE REGICIDE,
As ſet forth in the affidavit of
JOHN LONDON, Apr. 20, 1678.

Publiſhed from the original in the office of the Secretary of State of New-York,

BY

FRANKLIN B. HOUGH, M. D.

With other documents on the ſame ſubject among the State Papers of Connecticut.

"They did not regard them as Traitors, but as unfortunate ſufferers in the noble cauſe of civil Liberty, proſtrated by the Reſtoration, and again loſt and overwhelmed in the return and irreſiſtable inundation of Tyranny."

PRESIDENT STILES.

ALBANY,
WEED, PARSONS & CO.
M. DCCC. LV.

3

THE DEPOSICON

OF

JOHN LONDON

of Windsor in Connecticutt Apr. 20, 1678.

[N. Y. Colonial MSS., Vol. xxix, Secretary's Office, Albany, N. Y.]

John London of Winsor neare Hartford in the Colony of Conecticutt in New England, aged about fifty yeares, deposeth That Joseph Bull Sen'r (comonly called Capt Bull,) of Hartford, hath for severall yeares past (& for ought hee knowes still doth) kept privately Coll Goffe, at his owne house there, or his sons, hee goeing by the name of Mr Cooke; And that Whaley lived & dyed at Hadley in those parts, & was buryed in the buryeing place there. That being certifyed of the above Goffes aboade, in the month of May laſt, hee the deponent, together with Robert Howard of Winſor aforeſd (who profeſſeth phiſick) went to the houſe of the ſaid Bull, where they ſaw him & having formerly knowne him in England the deponent was well ſatisfyde that hee was the ſame man which ſd Dr. Howard did alſo affirme to him, as hee had done afore, hee being the firſt diſcoverer of his being there unto him.

That the ſaid Dr Howard did alſo informe him the deponent, that the Trade driven by ſd Bull or his Children, in Goods or Merchandize, was on the behalfe of ſd Goffe, & that Mr. James Richards of Hartford, brought over a good cargoe for the use of ſd Goffe about two yeares agoe.

That the deponent being so aſſured of ye ſaid Goffes aboade as before, in the ſame month of May, thinking it his duty, hee did call about & contrive which way to apprehend him, reaſonably ſuppoſing by Mr Richards acting for him, being a member of the Independent Church & a principall Magiſtrate there, that the authority would not countenance him, but the diſcovery to them would rather tend to his Ruine. The deponent therefore thought it convenient to adviſe wth & haue aſſiſtance of ſome other persons to ſeize vpon & bring the ſaid Goffe to this place & ſo diſclosed the ſame to one Thomas Powell his neighbour, who promiſt to aſſiſt the deponent therein, but no ſooner had the deponent diſcovered his knowledge & reſolucon to the ſd Powell, but hee privily went downe to Hartford upon a Saturday & gave informacon agnſt him, to Major Talcott & Capt Allen. That hee the deponent was goeing away to New Yorke having his horſe ready, on Monday following, but intended to ſurprize Coll. Goffe & carry him away with him. That the night following the ſd Powell returned to Winſor with the Marſhall Graves who about breake of day came to the depts houſe & knock't & called to him to ariſe.

The ſd dept knowing the Marſhallss voice aſkt' him what hee would have & what was the matter. The Marſhall anſwere'd that the dept muſt gett up, for the Gent. at Hartford had ſent to ſpeake with him: Whereupon the deponent aroſe & went with them to Hartford, where when they arrived, they went firſt to Major Talcotts, & from thence together to Capt Allens.

At the deponents coming there Capt Allen aſk't him when hee went to New York. The dept replyed, hee did not know but if hee had any buiſneſſe to comand him, & would pay him for it, hee was ready to goe preſently Capt Allen ſaid not hee but demanded him, if hee the dept had not appointed to goe thither on Monday, upon the depts saying hee knew nothing of it, Powell was call'd in then a paper was taken off the Table which Capt Allen ſaid hee woulde reade to him, if hee would hear it. The depont replyde that hee came to heare what they had to alleadge agſt him having ſent for him upon ye Sabbath day, fetching him out of his houſe, as a Traytor or Malefactor.

Then Capt Allen read the paper or charge given in agſt the dept by Thom: Powell relating what the dept had ſd unto him. Whereupon the dept put them upon the proofe of it Powells charge being alleadged. The dept replyde hee was but a ſingle Teſtimony, & likewiſe was an idle drunken fellow, & no heed to be given to what hee ſd, & the depont being in paſſion threatened the ſaid Powell that if hee could not have his remedy at Law agſt him hee would take his owne ſatiſfation.

Thereupon the depont being diſmiſt' he returned home.

Not long after Majr Talcott & Capt Allen came to Windſor to ſeeke for other Informacon agſt the dept but finding none lett the matter fall, yet charged the dept not to depart out of the County without a speciall Licence.

That at the ſame time when the ſd Major Talcott & Capt Allen were then there the depont told the ſd Major Talcott & Capt Allen & others preſt publickely, that hee the depont knew that they kept & concealed Coll: Goffe amongſt them, & that hee could when hee pleaſed lay his hand on his ſhoulder; To which they replyde the dept was miſtaken, for Goffe was long ſince dead, & charged the dept to bee a Traytor to their Colony & deſerved to bee hanged for conſpiring agſt them.

That afterwards the depont made a ſhip to goe off to Boſton under pretence of taking a horſe to ſell there, from thence hee ſhip't himſelfe for Maryland to his brother Major Ambroſe London living at Annemeſſick, in Somerſett County & there gave this Informacon upon oath to his ſd brother, Collonell Stevenſon, & Collonell Colburne, deſiring it might bee ſent into Engl'd, which they promis't. From thence the depont came to the Whorekill, & ſo hither. And further ſaith not.

Sworne before mee by the aforeſd John London, in New Yorke, the 20th day of Apr 1680:

Matthias Nicolls, *Sec'y.*

[Upon the receipt of the above intelligence Gov Andros addreſſed the following letter to the Governor of Connecticut, which with the accompanying documents are among the State papers of Connecticut Miscellaneous. Vol. i, Doc. 1, 2.]

Hon'ble S'rs.—Being informed by Deposicons taken upon Oath that Coll Goth hath been and is still kept and Concealed by Capt. Joseph Bull and his sonns in the Towne of Hartford under the name of Mr Cooke The sd Goth and Coll Whaley (who is since dead in yor parts) hauing been persued as Traitors, that I may not be wanting in my duty, doe hereby giue you the above intimacon, noe wayes doubting of yor loyalty in euery respect and remaine Hon'ble Srs. Your affectionate neighbor and humble servant. E. Andross.

New Yorke May 18th, 1680.

Superſcription—

For the Honoble John Leete Eſqr Governor & the Aſſiſtants of His Maties Collony of Connecticutt, att Hartford. Theſe. For his Maties ſpeciall ſervice.

MATTHIAS NICOLLS, *Sec'y.*

On the face of the letter in the handwriting of Sec'y. Allyn.

Preſently upon receipt of this letter, June 10th, '80, the Gour. Major Talcott & the Secretary being (when they receiued the letter) together, ordered the Secretary to send forth a warrant to the conſtables of Hartford to make ſearch for ſd Col. Goff in the letter metioned which was don accordingly before we parted. The copy of ye warrn.

To the Conſtables of Hartford. Whereas Sr. Edmond Andross Governor of N: Yorke by his letters to us juſt now receiued hath certifyed to us that Captn Jos. Bull & his ſonns of this Town doe conceale Col: Goffe under the name of Mr. Cooke, theſe are therefore in his Maties. name to will & require you and ſtrictly to charge and command you upon ſight hereof to make diligent ſearch in the houſes barns out houſes & all places therein for the ſayd Col: Goffe, & if you find him or them or any ſtranger in their or either of their houses you are to aprehend & in ſafe custody to convay them to the Governor, that they may be examind & diſpoſed of according to His Ma'-ties pleaſure formerly declared to us, & you are alſo to make search in all places wth in your limits where there may be any (or the least) ſuſ-ſpition that they may be hid or concealed, & you are to make return of the ſeruing hereof to the Governor vnder your hands, hereof you may not fayle as you will answer the contrary at your perill. Dated in Hartford June 10th, 1680, p order of ye Govr. &c.

ſigned p. JOHN ALLYN, *Secret'ry.*

REPLY TO ANDROSS'S LETTER.

Hartford, June 11th, 1680:

Hon'ble Sr :--Athough we muſt acknowledg o'r engagement vnto your Honor for giuing vs intimation of what had been offerd to your ſelfe reſpecting his Maties ſeruice (we ſhould haue taken it well had your Honor been pleaſed to haue giuen vs an acco't. of the names of the informers (which yet we desire you would be pleased to doe speedily) & we doubt not but to giue you sufficient sattisfaction, to clear it vp that we are much abused by those falls reports, concerning the good people of this place. For the prsent we know not how to acknowledg any thankes to the informers, who (by the effect) seem to haue acted under gross mistakes (possibly) to delude your Honor & cast reproach upon orselues of this place, for that we being upon a solemne occasion together when we receiued your letter, and information therein, we forthwith dispatcht a speciall warrant to or constables & marshall, to make a dilligent search after the person mentioned, whoe being upon oath, returned they had with all care & dilligence made the ſayd ſearch but could find no ſuch perſon as was mentioned, nor any ſtranger that in the leaſt could be ſuſpected to be any ſuch perſon: After the ſearch o'r people were amuſed that any ſuch thing could be ſuſpected at Hartford: But the father of lyes is o'r enemie & doth inſtigate his inſtruments to maligne this poore Colony, but we hope the Father of lights will vindicate vs in his due time, & we pray your Honors neighbourly charatie in the meane ſpace, with due witness bearing againſt all that endeavoure to abuſe with falls news & ſtories, as is done by o'rſelues in ſuch caſe, otherwiſe enough of ſuch matters had not been wanting againſt neighbours to rays bad blood by ill perſons betwixt ſuch as deſire to mayntaine good correſpondency with o'r profeſſed freinds that are neerly ſcituate to vs in this wilderneſſe, we haue not to ad but o'r reſpects to your Honor & that we are Hono'ble Sr.

Your affectionate freinds & humble ſervants, The Governor & Aſſiſts preſent,

p their order ſigned

JOHN ALLYN *Sec'ry*.

Theſe for the Hon'ble Sr EDMUN ANDROSS Knt. & Gov'r of his royall highness territories in America, at forte James in N. Yorke.

www.ingramcontent.com/pod-product-compliance
Lightning Source LLC
LaVergne TN
LVHW020635110826
845149LV00004B/1213

9781418191375